Easter Traditions around the World

by M. J. Cosson • illustrated by Elisa Chavarri

The Child's World®

Published by The Child's World®
1980 Lookout Drive • Mankato, MN 56003-1705
800-599-READ • www.childsworld.com

Acknowledgments
The Child's World®: Mary Berendes, Publishing Director
Red Line Editorial: Editorial direction
The Design Lab: Design
Amnet: Production

Design elements: Loskutnikov/Shutterstock Images

Photographs ©: Shutterstock Images, Cover, Title, 5, 29; Timothy Craig
Lubcke/Shutterstock Images, 9; Stephane Bidouze/Shutterstock Images, 11;
LiliGraphie/Shutterstock Images, 13; Gabriel Nardelli Araujo/Shutterstock
Images, 14; ShopArtGallery/Shutterstock Images, 15; iStockphoto, 21;
Roberto A Sanchez/iStockphoto, 23; Charles Dharapack/AP Images, 27

ISBN 9781614734260
LCCN 2012946511

Printed in the United States of America
Mankato, MN
November, 2012
PA02145

About the Author

M. J. Cosson has written many books for children. She lives in the Texas hill country with her husband, two dogs, and one cat. Easter has always been her favorite holiday. As a child, it brought new clothes for church, Easter-egg cakes from a friend's bakery, and a special coconut-filled chocolate egg.

About the Illustrator

Elisa Chavarri is a Peruvian illustrator who works from her home in Alpena, Michigan, which she shares with her husband, Matt, and her cat, Sergeant Tibbs. She has previously illustrated *Fly Blanky Fly*, by Anne Margaret Lewis, and *Fairly Fairy Tales*, by Esmé Raji Codell.

Table of Contents

Chapter One

Easter and the Spring

Easter is a very old holiday. It takes place when spring begins. Baby animals are born and trees get their leaves in spring. New plants pop up from the ground, and flowers bloom.

People always **celebrate** Easter on a Sunday. The date of Easter changes from year to year. It happens on the first Sunday after the first full moon after the first day of spring. This is in either March or April.

Easter is the most important holiday in the Christian religion. Christians believe the son of God, Jesus Christ, died on the Friday before Easter. They believe he was **resurrected** from the dead two days later, on Easter Sunday. Christians celebrate this as a message of God's love for his people.

This stained glass window shows Jesus's resurrection.

Chapter Two

Eggs and Rabbits

One **symbol** of Easter is the egg. The egg has been a symbol of life for a long time. For Christians, the egg is also a symbol of Jesus's resurrection. People dye and decorate eggs for Easter. Many people do not eat eggs or meat for 40 days before Easter. This time is called Lent. Eggs became a special present on Easter.

Another symbol is the rabbit. People thought rabbits had more babies than other animals. So the rabbit became a symbol of new life and rebirth.

Children look forward to a visit from the Easter bunny. The Easter bunny brings baskets full of candy or other gifts. It hides colored eggs for children to find.

People of different countries and beliefs have made their own **traditions**. Many traditions are celebrated in more than one country. Easter traditions are joyful, beautiful, funny, surprising, and often tasty.

Chapter Three

Easter in Australia

Australians celebrate Easter in March or April. But Easter is during Australia's fall. Australia is in the Southern **Hemisphere**. Fall comes to the Southern Hemisphere when spring comes to the Northern Hemisphere.

A favorite Easter treat is the hot cross bun. This sweet bun is made with spices and dried fruit. Australians also eat chocolate hot cross buns. The cross on top of the bun is a symbol of Easter. The Christian Bible says that Jesus died on a cross. The hot cross bun first came from England. English people moved to Australia and baked buns in their new home.

The Easter bunny or the Easter bilby brings eggs on Easter morning. The bilby is an Australian mammal. It has big ears and a long tail. Children also enjoy eating chocolate bilbies on Easter.

Chapter Four

Easter in England

English people eat hot cross buns before Easter. The bread is sweet and spicy. The buns have frosting crosses on top.

English children play the egg-picking game. Each of two players holds an egg in his or her hand. They cover almost the whole egg. Then the players crack the egg tips together. The player whose egg does not crack is the winner. He or she then gets an egg from the other player.

Chapter Five

Easter in France

In France, children believe church bells bring Easter eggs and other treats. French Easter stories say all the church bells fly away on the Thursday before Easter. They fly to the city of Rome in Italy. From Thursday until Easter Sunday, the church bells in France are quiet.

The bells fly back on Easter morning. As they fly by, they drop Easter eggs and candy for children. Then the bells ring once again.

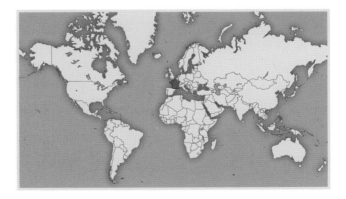

Chapter Six

Easter in Germany

Germans celebrate the end of winter in the weeks before Easter. In some places tall poles are decorated with Easter symbols. They are placed near the front door of people's houses. Later they are carried to church.

The Thursday before Easter is Green Thursday. Children eat meals of all green foods. An old story says that anyone who does not eat green on this day will become a donkey.

Many believe the traditions of Easter eggs and the Easter bunny came from Germany. On the night before Easter, children make a nest for the Easter bunny to leave eggs. On Easter morning, children enjoy real eggs. They also eat eggs made of **fondant** with a chocolate coating. Another treat is an egg filled with sweets and small toys.

Chapter Seven

Easter in Ghana

Most Christians in Ghana spend the four-day weekend at a church camp or in church. Many families celebrate the Monday after Easter with a picnic. Some families go to the beach.

A paragliding event takes place in the Kwahu Mountains in eastern Ghana. Paragliders jump from airplanes wearing parachutes. They glide to the ground. Paragliders from around the world come to compete. People gather to watch the colorful gliders fly through the sky.

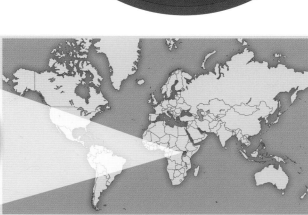

Chapter Eight

Easter in Italy

Italian children and grown-ups enjoy hollow chocolate Easter eggs with a surprise inside. They also eat *colomba* (ko-LOME-bah) bread in the shape of a dove. Colomba means "dove."

New clothes are an important part of Easter morning. These might be dresses, shirts, or pairs of shoelaces. Wearing something new is a way to celebrate new life.

Chapter Nine

Easter in Mexico

In Mexico, almost everyone takes the week before Easter off from work. This week is called *Semana Santa*, or Holy Week. Each day has special **ceremonies**. Many Mexicans go on vacation this week, too. They go to the beach or visit family.

People go to church on Easter Sunday. Then they celebrate with feasts and **fiestas**. Some towns put on plays about the life of Jesus. Other towns have fireworks. The fireworks might make castles, crowns, flowers, and other beautiful pictures in the sky.

Chapter Ten

Easter in the Netherlands

Dutch children decorate a wooden post with oranges, raisins, and figs. It might have eggshells, chocolate eggs, and small cakes, too. It might also have paper flags and little swans or birds. On the Sunday before Easter, children carry their post in one hand. They carry an empty basket in the other. They ask family and neighbors for eggs.

Children search for colored eggs hidden outside on the Monday after Easter. They put each egg they find in a basket. When the basket is full, the child finds a partner. Then the partners play the egg-knocking game. First the partners match egg colors. Then they knock the eggs together. The person whose egg does not break wins. She or he gets to keep all the eggs in both baskets.

Chapter Eleven

Easter in Poland

In Poland, people make *pisanki* (pee-SON-key), or special Easter eggs. The first step is to draw on the eggshell with hot wax. Then the artist dips the egg in dye. The part of the egg that has wax on it stays white. Each egg can be two or more colors. The artist can paint more wax designs between colors. The new dyes will not stick to the wax.

When the egg is done, the artist melts off the wax with a candle flame. Next the egg is polished. The final step is to punch a tiny hole in both ends of the egg. Blowing gently through one hole forces the insides out through the other hole. Pisanki are displayed in homes. People give the beautiful eggs as gifts.

The Monday after Easter is called *Dyngus* (DIN-goose) Day. Boys and men drench girls and women with water. The next day, the girls and women drench the boys and men!

Chapter Twelve

Easter in Spain

In Spain, the week before Easter is a time for quiet. Peaceful parades and ceremonies are held. Most stores and businesses are closed. People wear dark colors before Easter. They are mourning Jesus's death.

On Easter morning the world comes alive again. Parades have floats decorated with flowers and candles. People wear bright party clothes to bullfights and fiestas. On Easter people can eat meat again. They have a big feast.

Easter eggs and the Easter bunny are not well known in Spain. Some candy shops sell chocolate eggs. Some children receive *hornazo* (or-NAH-zoh) bread. It is a round bun with a hard-boiled egg and sausage baked into it.

Most of Spain's customs are also practiced in Portugal, Central America, and South America.

Spanish children march in a ceremony at their church during Holy Week.

Chapter Thirteen

Easter in Sweden

Before Easter it is time for spring-cleaning. Families scrub and clean their homes. They decorate them with yellow flowers such as daffodils. Yellow is the color of Easter in Sweden.

Weeks before Easter people cut birch branches and decorate them. As the weeks go by, new leaves grow on the branches.

On Easter eve, little girls dress up as the Easter Witch. They have red cheeks and black soot on their noses and eyebrows. Each girl wears a long skirt, a bright shirt, and a scarf. The girls parade around. They carry copper pots to collect eggs.

People light big Easter fires near the center of towns. They dance, shout, and sing to celebrate Easter.

Chapter Fourteen

Easter in the United States

People from countries around the world have moved to the United States. They brought their Easter traditions with them. Many traditions have stayed the same. Some have changed over the years.

Many children in the United States color Easter eggs. Children also hunt for Easter eggs before Easter and on Easter morning.

The German Easter hare became the Easter bunny. The bunny leaves eggs and baskets for children on Easter morning.

There is egg rolling at the White House in Washington DC. Children gather on the lawn on the Monday after Easter. This tradition has taken place for more than 150 years. Other communities around the country hold egg rolls, too.

In England, bun sellers on street corners and children have sung this rhyme for ages.

Hot Cross Buns

Hot cross buns! Hot cross buns!
One a penny, two a penny,
Hot cross buns!
If you have no daughters,
Give them to your sons!
But if you have none of these merry little elves,
Then you may keep them all to yourselves!
One a penny, two a penny,
Hot cross buns!

Coloring Easter Eggs

Ingredients

hard-boiled eggs (have a grown-up
  do this)
white crayon
egg carton
bowls, one for each color
spoon
water
vinegar
food coloring

Directions

1. Make designs on the eggs with a crayon. The designs will be uncolored because the dye will not stick to the wax.
2. Put the eggs in the bowls.
3. Cover the eggs with water so no parts of the eggs are above the water.
4. Add one teaspoon of vinegar to each bowl.
5. Add a different color food coloring to each bowl. The more you add, the darker the eggs will be.
6. When the eggs are colored, use a spoon to remove them from the dye. Place them back in the egg carton and put it in the refrigerator.

Glossary

celebrate (SEL-uh-brate) To celebrate is to observe or take notice of a special day. Many people celebrate Easter.

ceremonies (SER-uh-moh-nee) Ceremonies are events that are organized to celebrate special things. There are many ceremonies at Easter time.

decorate (DEK-uh-rate) To decorate is to make something pretty. We will decorate Easter eggs tomorrow.

fiestas (fee-ES-tuh) Fiestas are celebrations or festivals. We have fiestas at Easter.

fondant (fahn-dunt) Fondant is a flavored sugar paste. People fill chocolates with fondant.

hemisphere (HEM-i-sfeer) A hemisphere is half of the earth, either north or south of the equator. Australia is in the Southern Hemisphere.

resurrected (res-ur-EK-tid) Someone who is resurrected has come back from the dead. Easter celebrates when Jesus was resurrected.

symbol (SIM-buhl) A symbol is an object or sign that stands for something else. A heart is a symbol for love.

traditions (truh-DISH-uns) Traditions are ways of thinking or acting communicated through culture. Many families have Easter traditions.

Learn More

Books

Heligman, Deborah. *Holidays Around the World: Celebrate Easter: With Colored Eggs, Flowers, and Prayer.* Washington, DC: National Geographic, 2010.

Tegen, Katherine. *The Story of the Easter Bunny.* New York: HarperCollins, 2005.

Web Sites

Visit our Web site for links about Easter traditions around the world: **childsworld.com/links**

Note to Parents, Teachers, and Librarians: We routinely verify our Web links to make sure they are safe and active sites. So encourage your readers to check them out!

Index